Auto Deploy your Private Containerized Applications

Table of Contents

Preface

Following my previous book on building your private Kubernetes cluster on your own infrastructure, I wanted to continue the series on ideas around which setup might be interesting to help our developers get applications faster and more easily to production when the code is ready or fast deployment for testing. The concepts and infrastructure are the same for both.
We will show how to set up a private artifact repository for your applications and a build server and what you need to do to interconnect them with your cluster and development machine.

After that, we will have some walkthrough examples to deploy your application to your cloud.

All the tools are interchangeable with some public offerings or other alternatives that you might want to install so each step will be clearly separated from each other so you would know where you can plug-in a different option.

Note that all examples will be based on a Git source code repository and we will assume that the deployment are done in a Kubernetes cluster.

Who should read this book?

If you want to know more about some options on how to set up a deployment pipeline from code to Kubernetes cluster, this book is definitively an option. But it can help for any of the different step involved:
-    Private repository for your jar, war, npm or docker container
-    How to build a container from your application code
-    Automatically build code and deploy the result

Why I wrote this book?

After finishing my previous book on setting up the infrastructure to run our software, it seems to be a logical step to show how you could interact with the infrastructure without going through manual steps. So, I thought I would also share my experiences on how we automate our release process. I also thought that, even if it was based from our existing infrastructure, it could be helpful for other type of infrastructures.

Introduction

In many organizations, internal rules or, in some cases, laws would forbid you to use external offerings for your code. You wouldn't be allowed to use clouds as many others can. Might it be for privacy or security reasons. I have personally worked on solution for a customer that had laws in place requiring the physical location of the server in use for any part of the solution to be located in their country. This was a country which did not have any cloud providers located in so we could not use AWS, Azure or GCP.

So, in some cases, it might be good to know how to set up the tools you will need in your own infrastructure. This might include the source code, artifact registry, building server, servers where your application will run on, test environment, etc.

Our goal here is to have a solution that can auto detect changes in a source code repository and will trigger a build. Depending on the branch the code was pushed to, we will build the code and run the tests then publish the resulting artifact(s) and we will also deploy the application to our Kubernetes cluster if it comes from a specific branch. I am assuming here that you will have some strategies in place for feature branches and only one branch will be deployed to production (or branches based on patterns i.e. prod_*).

All software will be installed on a Linux machine that we assume meets the minimum requirements. Those will be mentioned in the relevant chapters. For each new software we will install, I will present the reason behind my choice. Note that all options presented are open source and free to use.
There are alternatives for all of them and some are easier to install and/or use but might be more expensive. I would also recommend using your existing infrastructure whenever possible. There is no need for feature duplication.

The command line example will be from a Debian based system (Ubuntu) so, if you are running on a Red Hat based or others, you might need to change some

command lines. i.e. apt-get would be yum and some package names might vary slightly. If you are unsure, you can run the commands from this book on your system and it will notify you if it is incorrect.
Manually installed packages will be located in the /opt directory

Which software do we need?

In this book, I will assume that we already have some source control management in place. I wrestled with the idea of showing how to set up one but couldn't find any good tool that were free and offer good functionality. You could set up git-scm on a server but wouldn't get Pull Request functionality and no UI to create new repositories. You could get Bitbucket server or GitHub Enterprise, but it gets expensive very fast. The only real alternative I could find was GitLab Core, but it is a huge all-in-one package that is not a way that I want to go towards. Now, that being said, if it is a solution that could work for you, it has almost all the pieces described in this book so you can check it out.

Now, from the source code, we will need something to build it, push the created artifact(s) to a repository and, eventually, publish the new code. We also want the artifact repository to be private. This means that it will be installed on our own infrastructure (not at a cloud provider) and will not allow anonymous access.

When all this is installed, we also need our tools to be able to use it. We will show how to set up NPM and maven to login to our private registry and the extra steps needed in the build server as well.

Note: During publishing of this book. GitHub changed their pricing and packaging on April 15, 2020. It now will offer unlimited private repositories in their free plan and will allow you to create an organization for free.

Private Artifact Repository

You might also say that we can get all this from free from central maven, npmjs and Docker hub. This is true and do not require any special configuration of any tools as there are predefined in their respective client. However, the free alternatives do not allow you to have any private repositories. Meaning that all will be opened with anonymous access. This might be good enough for you, but many organizations have the need to protect some of the applications they create.

To give you an idea to get private repositories in the default URLs, as per the time of writing this, npmjs and Docker hub will cost $7/month, maven does not offer this at all.

Since going through these solutions for those is pretty out-of-the-box, you basically need to create an account, pay and that will work, I will not go into these and focus on a private repository.

First, we need to decide which tool to use so let's think about what we need. Your requirements may vary but, since you are ready this, I will assume that Docker repository is one we may have in common. I will add maven and npm as they probably are 2 of the most common ones. All others will be a nice addition but not hard requirement.

If you do a search for this, you will probably find that there are only 2 real competitors for this: JFrog Artifactory and Sonatype Nexus. Both support a large amount of repository types that cover what we need and much, much more (NuGet, rpm (YUM), deb (APT), PyPI, Helm…). However, Artifactory only supports maven, Gradle and Ivy in the open source edition so you would need to pay minimum $2,950/year to access Docker and npm repository functionality.

So, our choice goes towards Nexus since all the repositories are available in the OSS platform.

Requirements

Nexus will run on most OS. Windows, Mac OS and Linux that will run 64-bit Java 8. Java 8 ONLY. Not Java 8 or newer. No other versions are supported.

It is highly recommended to run Nexus with its own dedicated user account. Nexus will not run as root. You will also want to set a higher file handle limit on *nix system. On linux, set it in the `/etc/security/limits.conf` by adding `nexus - nofile 65536` assuming that the username of the account running the application is nexus or in the system startup script.
There is a caveat on Ubuntu though. Ubuntu ignores the limit.conf for processes started by init.d. So, if you set Nexus up with init.d, you will need to edit the `/etc/pam.d/common-session` file and uncomment the line including pam_limits.so.
If you are using systemd, you can add the LimitNOFILE=65536 flag in the file. If you wish to use the Docker image, start it with `-ulimit nofile=65536:65536`.

CPU: 4 minimum and 8 recommended

Memory: minimum 8GB on the host, JVM heap size should be 2703 MB minimum but should not exceed 4 GB except when you have evidence that it is consistently utilized, and you have lengthy garbage collection. You should set the Xms and Xmx to the same value. You also must set the JVM direct memory flag (--XX:MaxDirectMemorySize) to minimum 2703 MB and maximum (host physical memory * 0,66) – JVM max heap.

The minimum requirements are enough for up to 20 repositories and 20 GB blobstore. If you want to go up to 50 repositories and around 200 GB store, you will need 16 GB physical memory. This would mean -Xms4G -Xmx4G --XX:MaxDirectMemorySize=6717M

Disk space is highly installation specific. When using Nexus, it is usually used as a proxy to search for other artifacts in central repositories. All those will be

cached and consume space. As we know, docker images takes a lot of space so it will probably take quickly up to 500 GB. In any case, you should have a filesystem that you can expand (i.e. use LVM on Linux).
There are also a couple of notes on the file system. Glusterfs is known to create split-brain and is very slow. You should also avoid FUSE based user space filesystems. If you want to use NFS for blob storage, use NFS v4 and do not use it for anything else than blob storage.

Supported browsers are Chrome, Firefox, Safari, Edge and IE 11. The policy is to support the latest version of all browser still supported by the manufacturer.

Installation

First, from the requirements we just described, we will need to create a nexus service user:

```
sudo useradd -M nexus
sudo usermod -L nexus
```

This adds a user without login capabilities into the server.

Then install JRE 8:

```
sudo apt-get install openjdk-8-jre
```

Now we can download the Nexus package from the official web site and unpack it.

```
cd /opt
sudo wget https://download.sonatype.com/nexus/3/latest-unix.tar.gz
sudo tar -zxvf latest-unix.tar.gz
```

This will result in 2 directories:
- nexus-<version number>: the software itself
- sonatype-work: the working directory

Now change ownership of these 2 to our nexus service user:

```
sudo chown -R nexus:nexus nexus-3.22.0-02/
sudo chown -R nexus:nexus sonatype-work/
```

I usually soft-link the resulting nexus-<version> to nexus. This is a totally optional step but recommended if you will use this installation over time.

```
sudo ln -s nexus-3.22.0-02/ nexus
```

It will simplify the eventual upgrade and some maintenance since, after upgrading, the base directory would change if you didn't do this in any script you have created.
This means that, to upgrade, you will just need to stop Nexus then download, unpack the new tar. Then change the soft-link and start nexus again. Do check release notes and upgrade notes for eventual breaking changes but I've upgrade all my v3 of nexus with the following simple commands

```
sudo service nexus stop
cd /opt
sudo wget https://download.sonatype.com/nexus/3/latest-unix.tar.gz
sudo tar -zxvf latest-unix.tar.gz
sudo chown -R nexus:nexus nexus-<new version number>/
sudo chown -R nexus:nexus sonatype-work/
sudo rm nexus
sudo ln -s nexus-<new version number>/ nexus
sudo service nexus start
```

Now, let's set the correct JVM flag based on the host memory. The default is set to the minimum requirements so, if you do not have more than 8 GB of memory, you can skip this step.

```
sudo vim /opt/nexus/bin/nexus.vmoptions
```

And change the Xms, Xmx and XX:MaxDirectMemorySize to the appropriate value as described under requirements.

As an example, if you have 16 GB, the values would be
-Xms4G
-Xmx4G
-XX:MaxDirectMemorySize=6717M

For 32 GB
-Xms4G
-Xmx4G
-XX:MaxDirectMemorySize=17530M

Since this is a server software, I will assume that we will run it as a service. There are multiple solutions to do so but I prefer using systemd. To do so, create a file called nexus.service in /etc/system/system

```
sudo vim /etc/systemd/system/nexus.service
```

with the following:

```
[Unit]
Description=nexus service
After=network.target

[Service]
Type=forking
LimitNOFILE=65536
ExecStart=/opt/nexus/bin/nexus start
ExecStop=/opt/nexus/bin/nexus stop
```

```
User=nexus
Restart=on-abort

[Install]
WantedBy=multi-user.target
```

Note that we use the soft-linked path, if you skipped this step, update the 2 paths accordingly. We also add the LimitNOFILE flag, so we have that covered. This is the main reason why I prefer this method.
Now, let's register, activate and start the service.

```
sudo systemctl daemon-reload
sudo systemctl enable nexus.service
sudo systemctl start nexus.service
```

Let it have some time to start then you can check it that http://<host.ip>:8081. Do not login yet!

Optional step: we will now set up a reverse proxy so that we can access nexus on normal HTTP(S) ports. There are 2 main web servers used on Linux to do so: Apache and nginx. Personally, I find nginx a little bit better (faster) as a proxy server but we will show them both. If you have one of them already installed, it is probably a bad idea to get the other as there are multiple port conflicts in the default installation. The scope of this book does not extend to the installation of these but, if you do not have any, it is a simple apt-get install command to run.

Here is the relevant configuration for Apache https:

```
ProxyRequests Off
ProxyPreserveHost On

<VirtualHost *:80>
    ServerName www.example.com
    ServerAdmin admin@example.com
```

```
  # Not needed if you are not using npm
  AllowEncodedSlashes NoDecode

  ProxyPass / http://localhost:8081/ nocanon
  ProxyPassReverse / http://localhost:8081/
  ErrorLog logs/www.example.com/error.log
  CustomLog logs/www.example.com/access.log common
</VirtualHost>
```

And for nginx:

```
http {
  proxy_send_timeout 120;
  proxy_read_timeout 300;
  proxy_buffering    off;

  server {
    listen    *:80;

    server_name  nexus.example.com;

    # allow large uploads of files
    client_max_body_size 1G;

    location / {
      # Use IPv4 upstream address instead of DNS name to
avoid attempts by nginx to use IPv6 DNS lookup
      proxy_pass http://127.0.0.1:8081/;
      proxy_set_header Host $host;
      proxy_set_header X-Real-IP $remote_addr;
      proxy_set_header X-Forwarded-For
$proxy_add_x_forwarded_for;
      #uncomment the following if your are running on
HTTPS (*:443)
      #proxy_set_header X-Forwarded-Proto "https";
    }
  }
}
```

Other solution might also be available to you NAT, HAProxy, etc. The idea is that we want to be able to access Nexus with the correct DNS name that will be used over time. This so all the configurations are set correctly. Changing path later on is quite painful.

Eventually, you would need to update your DNS but, now you can browse to the nexus host by name.

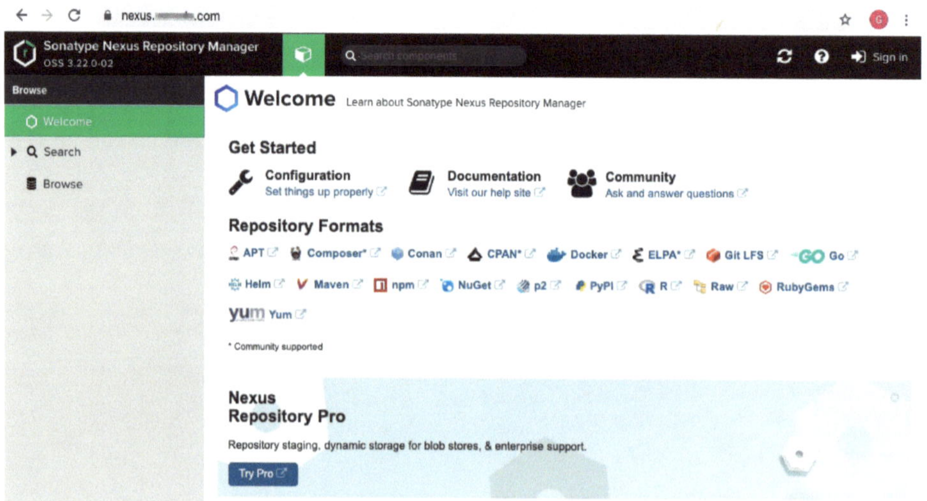

Basic configuration

Now let's login into the Nexus UI. Click "Sign in" at the top right. The default username is admin, and the default password is auto generated. You can fetch it from the file /opt/sonatype-work/nexus3/admin.password

You will get the setup wizard pop-up with a welcome screen. Next, you will have to set a password. This is the admin password, make it good! Next is whether you will allow anonymous access to this instance – I'll leave that up to you and it can be changed later as well. And you're done with the basic setup. There are, tough, a couple of extra steps I recommend:

1. Change the email address of the admin user:

Let's navigate to configuration -> Users -> Select admin

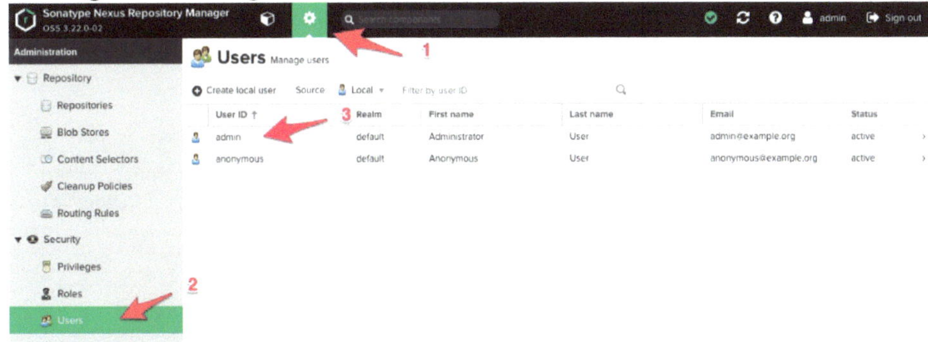

Change the email and save.

2. Configure Email Server can be found lower in the left pane. Fill it according to your SMTP server.

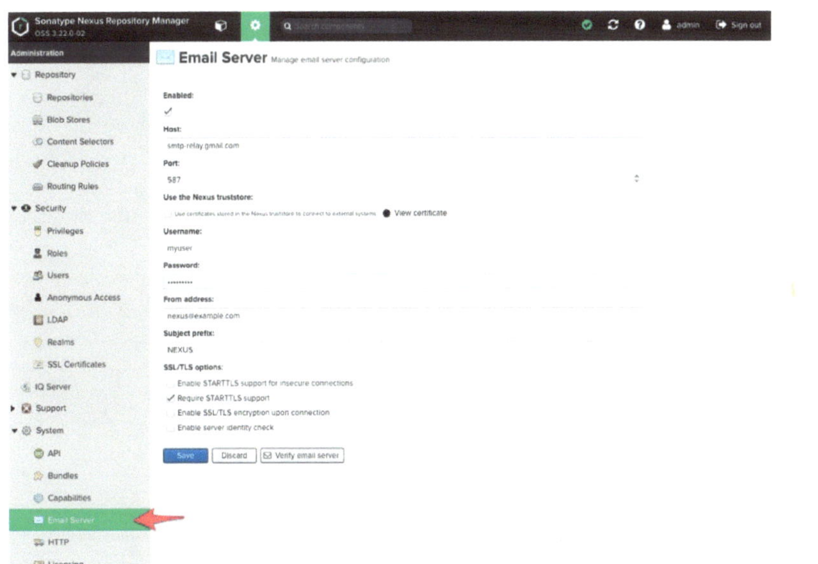

It is not a required step, but it will allow you to set up notifications by email and get the predefined system ones.

User directory integration (optional)

If you have an Active Directory or LDAP server, this is also the time to connect those. If you do so, also navigate to Security -> Roles -> Create role -> External role mapping -> LDAP (or AD)

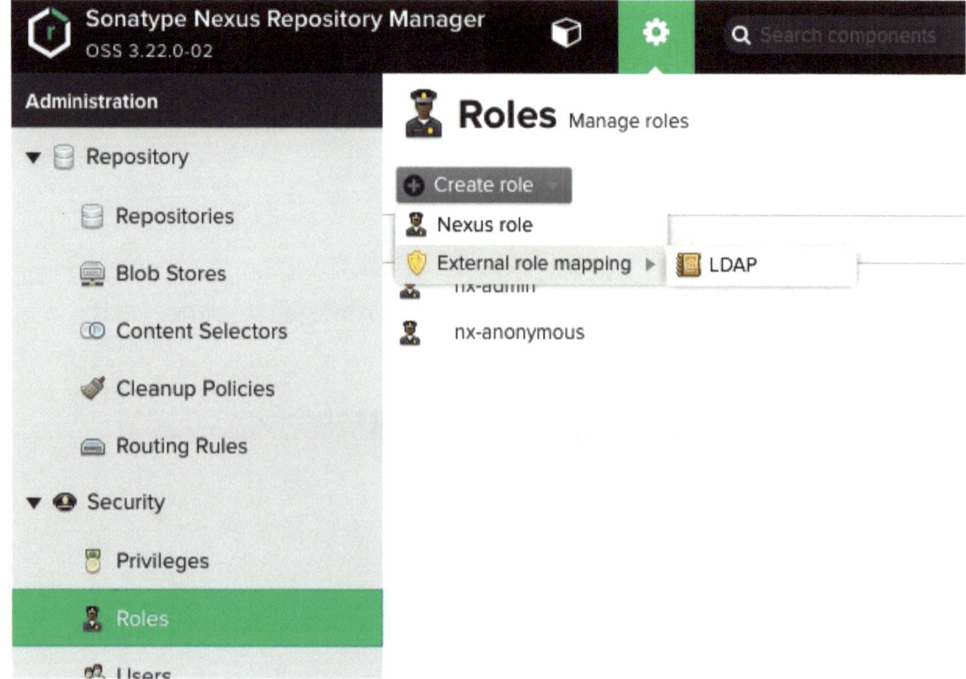

This will allow you to map your different LDAP groups to Roles and/or Privileges in Nexus.

Authentication Realm

There is one more thing we need to do. Navigate to the Realms configuration and add all Bearer Token Realm for the types you will want to configure a repository for. This is for the different clients to be able to login and due to the fact that the npm client handles it differently than the docker client.
If you have enabled anonymous access, this is not needed but you might want to do it anyway just in case you will disable it later.

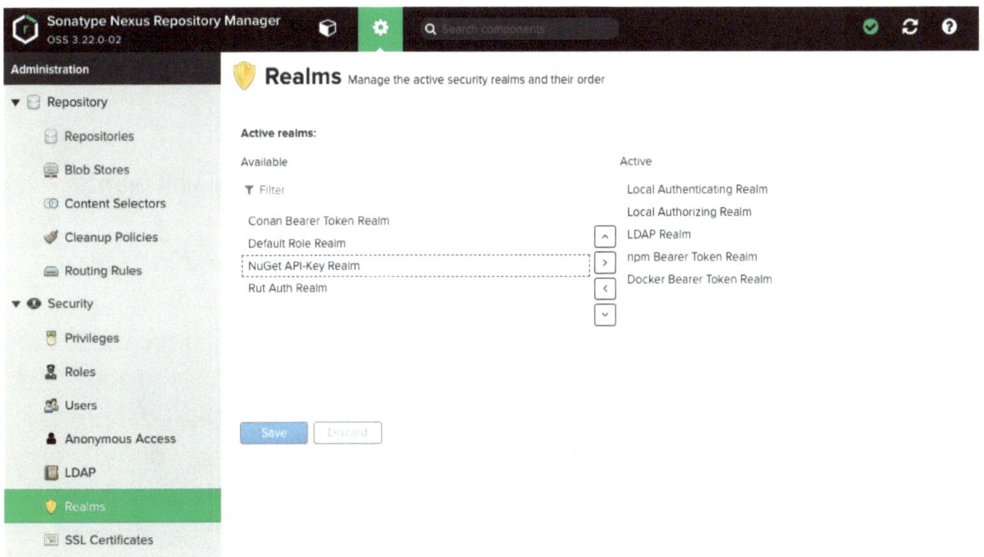

Repositories

The next step is to setup the different repositories we want in Nexus. By default, it has Maven and NuGet already configured. Note that there are 3 different types of repositories: proxy, hosted and group.

- A hosted repository is the one you actually deploy your artefacts to.
- A proxy repository is to connect to an external one. i.e. maven central. The artefacts you will fetch through Nexus to those proxied repositories will be cached locally.
- A group repository is what it says. A group of hosted and/or proxied repositories that will get a single name thus single URL. Usually the one you will fetch the artefacts from.

To give a maven representation, you will set your hosted repository for distribution management and the group for dependencies you will want to fetch. We will show this later.

The idea is that you will usually have one hosted repository (or 2 in case of maven to differ between release and snapshot), one or more proxied repositories to central or well-known third parties and you will have these in one group. This would be repeated for each format as you cannot group different formats. The client would not know how to handle this. i.e. npm CLI wouldn't understand a maven repository format. As a side note, I do not see any reason to have multiple groups within a format except if Nexus will be used by 2 different departments within your organization and they cannot have access to each other's artefacts.

So, let's create a set of repositories for Docker images. Go to the Repositories settings and click on Create repository.

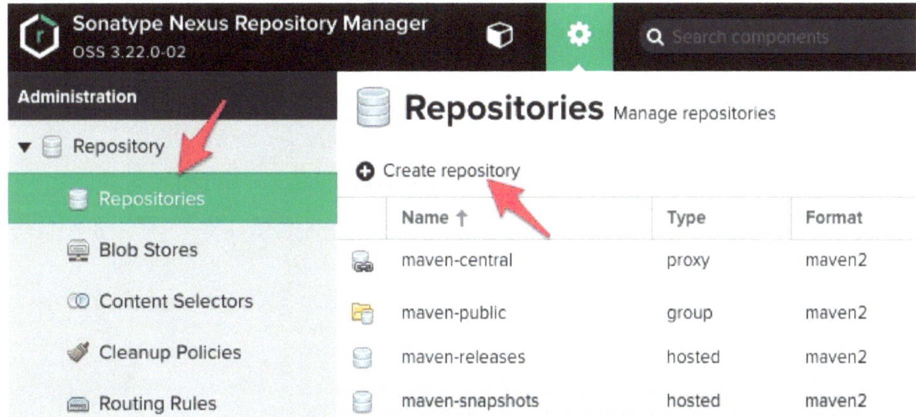

First, we will choose the Docker hosted for our own, give it a name (without space),
add a repository connector for HTTP and a port and Enable Docker V1 API to have all APIs available (there are still some that are not ported to V2 like search).

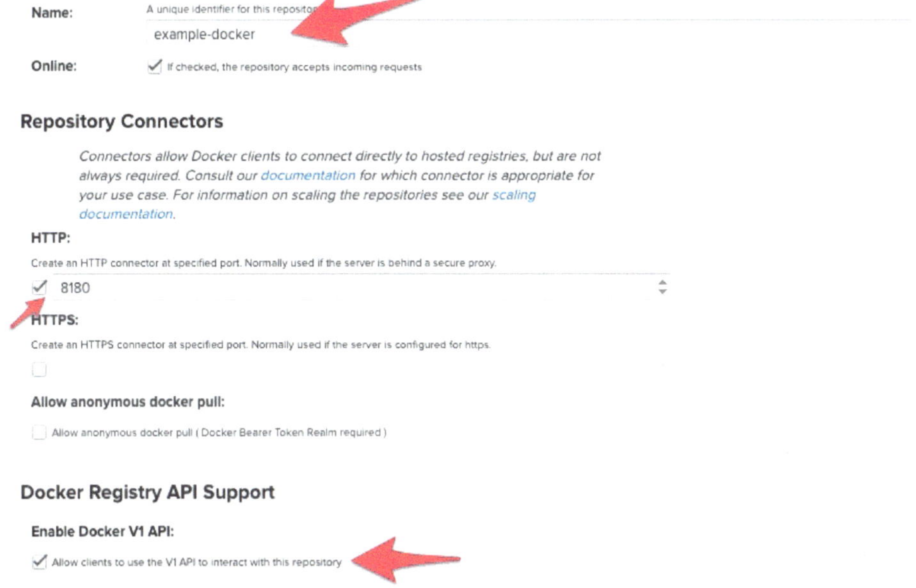

If you do not have a proxy in front of Nexus, change to an HTTPS connector.
Docker client requires an HTTPS connection to work so you will have to either
choose HTTPS here or have a proxy to handle SSL/TLS termination. I believe it
is easier to have a proxy as there are many tools to set up and renew
certificates in Apache or nginx but not for Nexus.
The configuration for the proxy is the same as above except for the port
number that you would need to update.
I usually set up docker registry on its own subdomain to avoid having non-
standard ports in use.

As the image URL of docker images would include the URL, we will not add the
proxy or group here. In addition, it would consume extensive amount of
storage if you have all base images cache here.
But let's do this for NPM. Again, go to create repository and choose the npm
proxy. Give it a name and set the remote storage. You can see the name is just
above the input field for NPM central.

Repositories / Select Recipe / Create Repository

Name:
A unique identifier for this repository

example-npm

Online:
☑ If checked, the repository accepts incoming requests

Proxy

Remote storage:

Location of the remote repository being proxied, e.g. https://registry.npmjs.org

https://registry.npmjs.org

Use the Nexus truststore:

☐ Use certificates stored in the Nexus truststore to connect to external systems ✸ View certificate

The rest I leave as default and we click the create repository button at the bottom. We create also a hosted repository for NPM with a name.

There is one configuration I want to draw your attention to: Deployment policy.

In maven, it is customary to allow redeploy on a snapshot repository but not on the release repository. NPM do not have this concept out-of-the-box. However, you could choose to create 2 repositories and let your build server handle this. i.e. master branch push to release repository, other branches push to a development repository. This might be handy if you have multiple teams working on a large project where one creates a library for the other and the second team needs the latest changes to test their own. I believe it is a bit far-fetched, so I usually only have one NPM repository and disable redeployment for NPM. Let the team create a new version if needed. Note that this setting is available for all types of hosted repositories.

Lastly, we create the npm group and add the 2 repositories as Members.

Maven is already defined by default, so we do not need to create them. However I think you should add the spring maven repository (http://repo.spring.io/release) to Nexus as a proxy and add it to the maven-public group. It will have many of the most used dependencies if, as myself, you are using Spring libraries.

Clients Configuration

NPM

To use our new private repository, we need to configure our client. The process is simple, we will:
1. Add our hosted repository
2. Login to the repository
3. Add our group
4. Login to the group repository

```
npm config set registry
https://nexus.example.com/repository/npm-group/
npm addUser
npm config set registry
https://nexus.example.com/repository/example-npm/
npm addUser
```

The addUser command will prompt you for your username, password and email. After this, you can run any npm command.

NOTE: This adds the new repository globally for the user. It will create a ~/.npmrc file. If you do not wish to do so and only do it for a specific project, you can move the file to the root catalogue of your project. I believe this would be relevant only if you have multiple private repositories.

If you get a 401-error saying: "Unable to authenticate, need: BASIC realm=Sonatype Nexus Repository Manager" when trying to run npm, you probably did not set the NPM Realm as described earlier.

One last thing. For the projects you want to publish to your private repository, just add

```json
  "publishConfig": {
    "registry":
"https://nexus.example.com/repository/example-npm/"
  }
```

to your package.json.

Maven

If you do not have it already, create a file called settings.xml under .m2 in your home catalogue.

```
vim ~/.m2/settings.xml
```

And add the following:

```xml
<?xml version="1.0" encoding="UTF-8"?>
<settings xmlns="http://maven.apache.org/SETTINGS/1.0.0 "
xmlns:xsi="http://www.w3.org/2001/XMLSchema-instance "

xsi:schemaLocation="http://maven.apache.org/SETTINGS/1.0.0
http://maven.apache.org/xsd/settings-1.0.0.xsd ">

    <mirrors>
        <mirror>
            <!--This sends everything else to /public -->
            <id>example-nexus</id>
            <mirrorOf>*</mirrorOf>

<url>https://nexus.example.com/repository/maven-
public</url >
        </mirror>
    </mirrors>


    <servers>
        <server>
```

```xml
                <id>osnode-example-snapshot</id>
                <username>username</username>
                <password>password</password>
            </server>
            <server>
                <id>osnode-example-release</id>
                <username>username</username>
                <password>password</password>
            </server>
              <server>
                <id>example-nexus</id>
                <username>username</username>
                <password>password</password>
            </server>
        </servers>
</settings>
```

The <mirrors> tag tells maven to go to our private repository instead of maven central. The <servers> tag will authenticate you for, in order, the snapshot repository, the release repository, the group and the docker repository. Note that the id used in the mirror must match one of the server tag defined below to fetch the correct credentials.

Now, in the projects you wish to publish your artefacts to this private repository, add the following in your pom.xml:

```xml
    <distributionManagement>
        <repository>
            <id>example-nexus-release</id>
            <url>https://nexus.example.com/repository/maven-releases/</url>
        </repository>
        <snapshotRepository>
            <id>example-nexus-snapshot</id>
            <url>https://nexus.example.com/repository/maven-snapshots/</url>
        </snapshotRepository>
    </distributionManagement>
```

Again, the id in your pom.xml MUST match the id in your settings.xml for maven to pick up authentication.

Docker

This is the really simple one. Just run

```
docker login https://docker.example.com
```

and it will prompt you for your username and password.

Build server

As usual, we first need to decide which build software we want to use. So, what are our requirements? At the very least, we want a tool to build Java projects, JavaScript/Typescript and that can handle integrations with our Source Control Management (SCM) so that builds are triggered by rules we can configure. We will favor Open Source and free tools over paying enterprise solutions. And maintainability of the software will also be important.
Other integrations will also be weight in, but we do not want to be stuck to a specific VCS for instance.

What options do we have?
There are a lot of tools available. Buddy, Jenkins, TeamCity, GoCD, Bamboo, Gitlab CI, CircleCI, Codeship, Buildbot, Nevercode are some examples. I did not go through others that do not have a certain amount of recognition I could find.
You might think that we have some missing here (like TravisCI) but there are not here as they are too tightly integrated with other tools for my taste (as far as I know, it will only work with GitHub and Bitbucket has just arrived in Beta only).
From the list above, I will do some cleaning up and focus on only the ones that provides a free version. Let's say goodbye to Buddy, Bamboo and Nevercode. I will also add CircleCI to this list as the free option restricts us to 1 build at a time.

Next, I will also pass on GitLab. If you would prefer an all-in-one solution, GitLab offers a comprehensive tool that bundles almost everything that you would need for developments. However, the free edition is limited, and it might not be enough for what you need. And, as I stated, I want to keep my options open for other tools integrations. I guess it might be possible to make it work with GitLab, but I don't see the point of having all these features if you will not use them.

To help us a bit further, I will also not go into Buildbot further. Simply because their web site is so bad that it requires a huge effort just to find a feature list. Codeship is a cloud-only provider and also very hard to find what you actually get on the free version from the documentation and which integrations it supports so I will not dig deeper into it either.

That leaves us with Jenkins, TeamCity and GoCD.

Let's take those tools through our list of requirements.
- All 3 supports any relevant SCM and have necessary built-in triggers to start building when we want them to.
- TeamCity is closed source but has a full featured free version and the other 2 are open source.
- Jenkins and GoCD offer packages for all major OSes while TeamCity is a tar or war file
- Jenkins has around 1500 integrations; TeamCity is just above 300 and GoCD is below 100

So, it seems that Jenkins is the winner here as the other 2 are losing points because of the number of integrations and TeamCity also because of the installation method.

I want to draw your attention on a couple of things though. GoCD is built with continuous deployment in mind and is relatively young so it might catch up in the future.
And TeamCity do offer a couple of nice feature/integration with IntelliJ IDE (both are from the same company) and can provide enterprise support if you buy it so it might be a good alternative.

Anyways, we will go with Jenkins as it seems to be the best alternative for us at the moment.

Requirements

First, get the easy part out of the way. We need Java 8 or 11.

Now, to the harder parts… Jenkins offers the possibility of running in a master/slaves combination where you can add multiple nodes. Each one could have different capabilities or have all of them being able to handle all type of jobs. So, based on that, I will assert that the official documentation saying 256 MB of RAM and 1 GB of drive space as minimum and recommending 1 GB+ of RAM and 50 GB+ of drive space, is to run the master and not many capabilities on the same server.

To give you an idea, I have been running a Jenkins server without any slaves for some time with 4 GB of RAM and 50 GB of disk space that has been running 20 Jobs without any issues.

Installation

We will add the official Jenkins apt repository and simply install it from the official packages. Just run:

```
wget -q -O - https://pkg.jenkins.io/debian/jenkins.io.key | sudo apt-key add -
curl -s https://packages.cloud.google.com/apt/doc/apt-key.gpg | sudo apt-key add -
sudo sh -c 'echo deb http://pkg.jenkins.io/debian-stable binary/ > /etc/apt/sources.list.d/jenkins.list'
echo "deb https://apt.kubernetes.io/ kubernetes-xenial main" | sudo tee -a /etc/apt/sources.list.d/kubernetes.list
sudo apt-get update
sudo apt-get install openjdk-11-jdk jenkins kubectl
```

This will install Java 11 as well as the LTS version of Jenkins as a service and start it. I also added kubectl CLI as we will use it later to deploy the images we build.

As Jenkins and Kubernetes are not publishing their software in the central Ubuntu repository and rather their own, we added the key for those so we do not get errors when apt check the signature of the packages.

As for Nexus, we will setup an Apache or nginx proxy in front. The configuration is exactly the same except that the port is 8080 instead of 8081 and we need to add one more flag in nginx:

```
proxy_redirect http://127.0.0.1:8080
https://jenkins.example.com
```

This is not required but Jenkins will give you some warnings if you don't.

Since we have an official package for our OS, the upgrade here will just be

```
sudo apt-get upgrade
```

As an extra step here, we will add Docker that we will use for building jobs later. First remove old versions of the software that comes from the OS repositories.

```
sudo apt-get remove docker docker-engine docker.io
containerd runc
```

You might not have all (or even any) installed but it is to avoid conflicts. Now add the official Docker repository:

```
curl -fsSL https://download.docker.com/linux/ubuntu/gpg |
sudo apt-key add -
sudo add-apt-repository "deb [arch=amd64]
https://download.docker.com/linux/ubuntu $(lsb_release -
cs) stable"
sudo apt-get update
```

```
sudo apt-get install docker-ce docker-ce-cli containerd.io
```

And add the daemon to startup

```
sudo systemctl enable docker
```

Since Docker daemon uses a Unix socket we need to add the Jenkins user to the docker group.

```
sudo usermod -aG docker jenkins
```

You might want to add your own user as well to test but it is not necessary.

N.B: If you still get errors that the builds cannot start the docker images and are sure that the Jenkins user is in the docker group, you might need to restart Jenkins.

Configuration

Now, you can navigate to the Jenkins URL with your browser of choice and it will take you through a simple wizard.

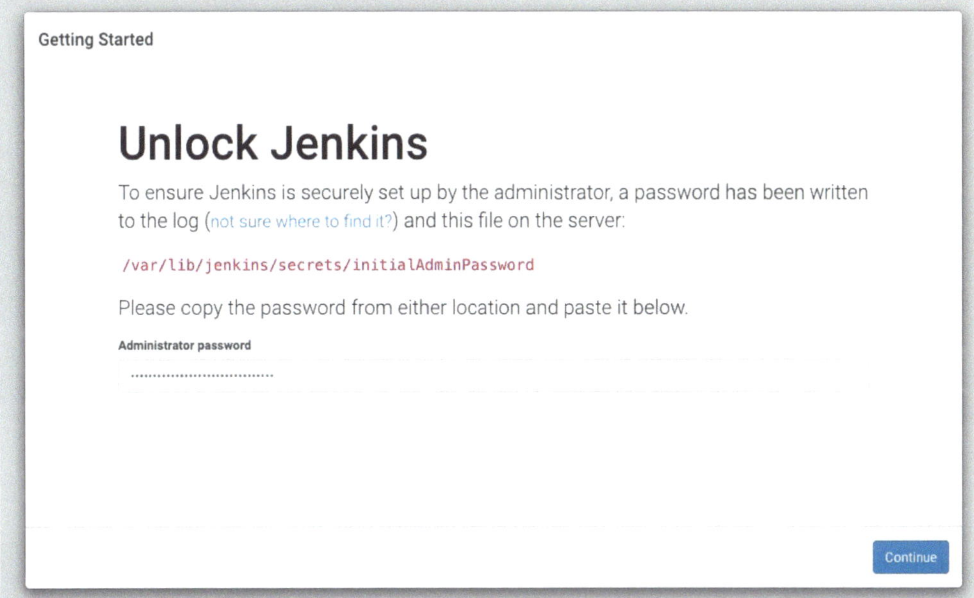

Fetch the password and click "Continue".

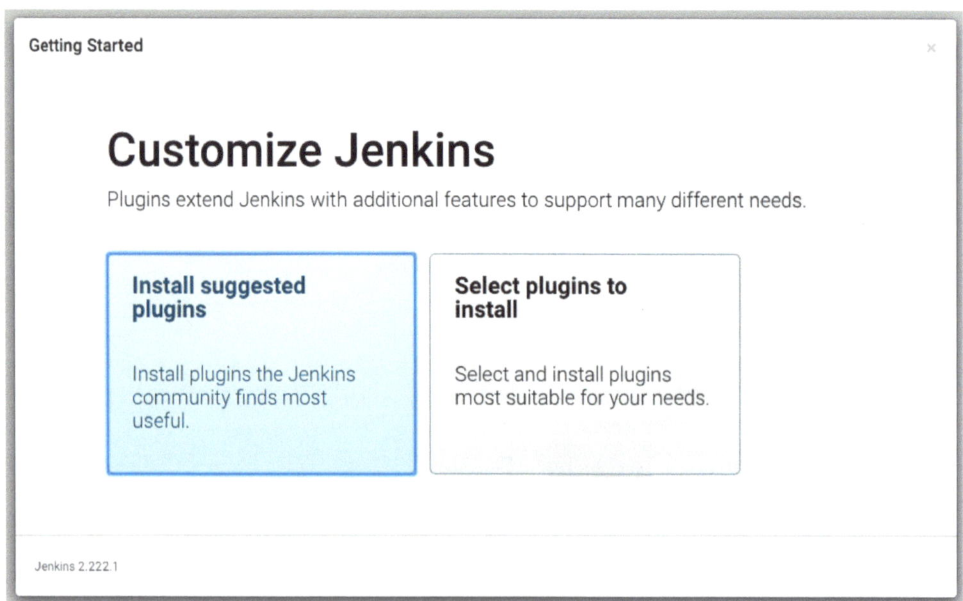

Click "Install suggested plugins" and Jenkins will now work for a minute setting those up and will take you to a screen to set up the first admin user.

I'll leave you to choose a strong password here. Click save and continue and the wizard will ask you to confirm the URL.

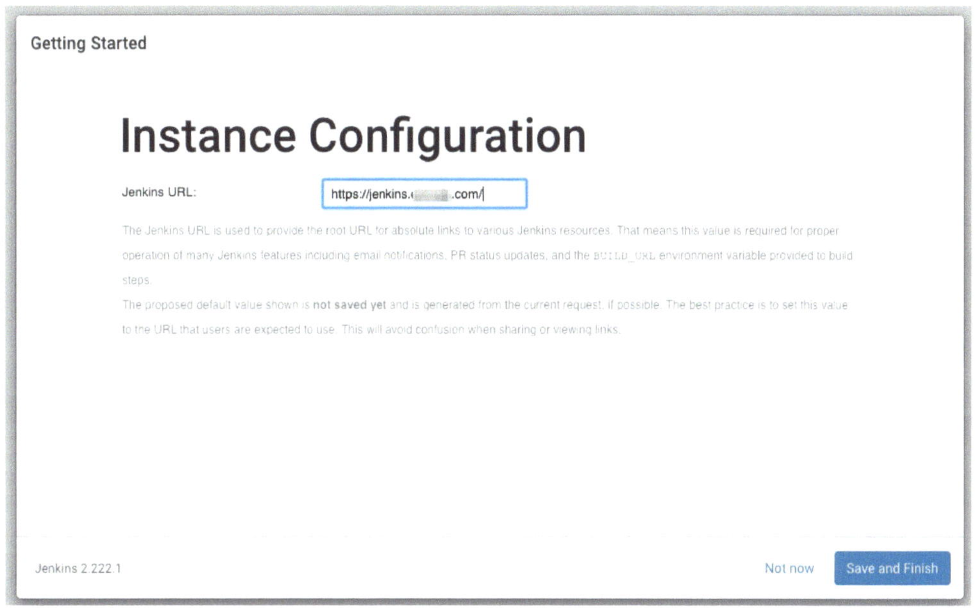

This needs to be the URL you will use in the end. If you have gone to the server through its IP, this would be auto-detected here but I would recommend setting an FQDN in any cases. Click "Save and Finish" and you will be taken to the dashboard.

Before moving forward, let's add a couple of plugins to our installation. You can find the plugin manager under Manage Jenkins > Manage Plugins

Then switch to the "Available" tab. We will add the Kubernetes CLI plugin to help us. Also, if you want to connect to Bitbucket (cloud or server), add the Bitbucket branch source plugin.

We will now configure our private repository for Jenkins. You could use an existing user for this but I prefer having better traceability so I will explain how to create a minimal role for system applications and a Jenkins user with that role attached.

First create a role in Nexus for Jenkins (and possibly others that should be able to read and write to the different repositories). To do so, navigate to the system configuration > Roles > Create role

Sonatype Nexus Repository Manager
OSS 3.22.0-02
geoffrey
Sign out
Administration
Repository
Repositories
Blob Stores
Content Selectors
Cleanup Policies
Routing Rules
Security
Privileges
Roles
Users
Roles Manage roles
Create role
Filter
Name
Source
Description
nx-admin
Nexus
Administrator Role
nx-anonymous
Nexus
Anonymous Role
1
2
3

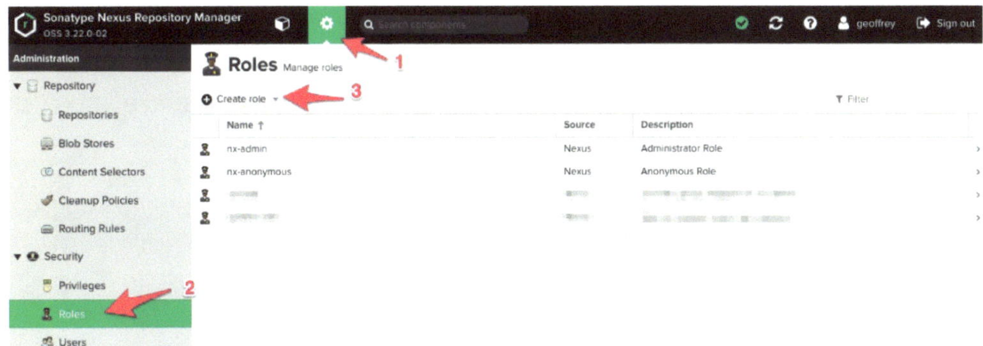

And fill the form like this:

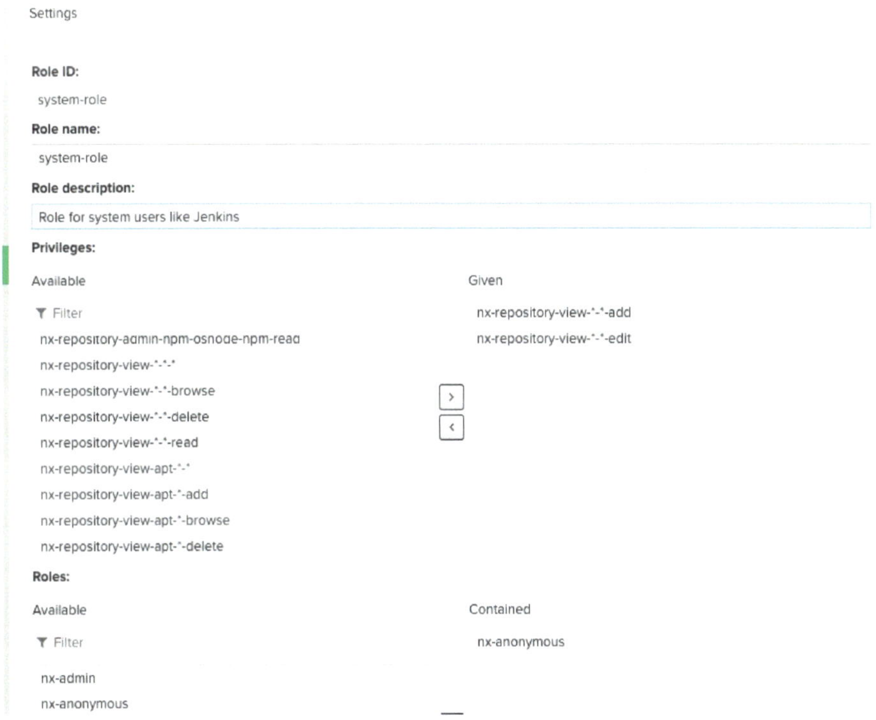

Settings
Role ID:
system-role
Role name:
system-role
Role description:
Role for system users like Jenkins
Privileges:
Available
Given
Filter
nx-repository-admin-npm-osnode-npm-read
nx-repository-view-*-*-*
nx-repository-view-*-*-browse
nx-repository-view-*-*-delete
nx-repository-view-*-*-read
nx-repository-view-apt-*-*
nx-repository-view-apt-*-add
nx-repository-view-apt-*-browse
nx-repository-view-apt-*-delete
nx-repository-view-*-*-add
nx-repository-view-*-*-edit
Roles:
Available
Contained
Filter
nx-admin
nx-anonymous
nx-anonymous

And save. Note that we've added the nx-anonymous role that has read permission and added write privileges for all repositories. You might want to add the "add" and "edit" privileges to specific repositories instead of all but, for this example, it is sufficient.

Now, just below the Roles management, you can find Users. Go there and click "Create local user"

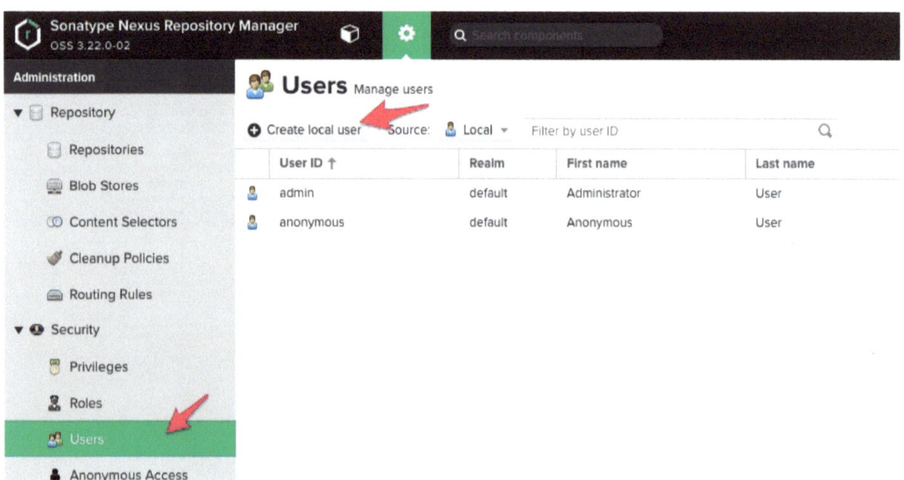

Now, we can setup our tools earlier on our Jenkins server for our Jenkins user. So you can, either switch to the Jenkins user and run the commands as earlier (you might need to install the software for npm), or run them locally and copy .npmrc to the Jenkins user home catalog. Note that the home catalogue of the Jenkins user is /var/lib/jenkins.

The last step is to load the configuration for our Kubernetes cluster in Jenkins. The simplest way is to create a file credentials. Go to Credentials then System.

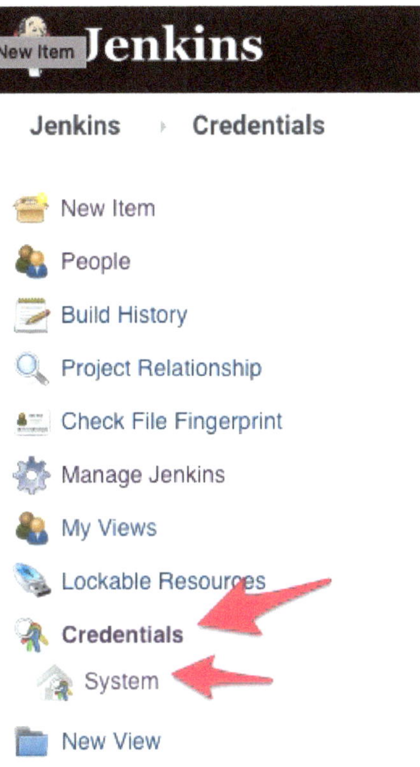

You will get a list with just one entry (on a new installation) saying Global Credentials and, here is the trick, you need to mouse over the link but click on triangle beside it (not the link itself).

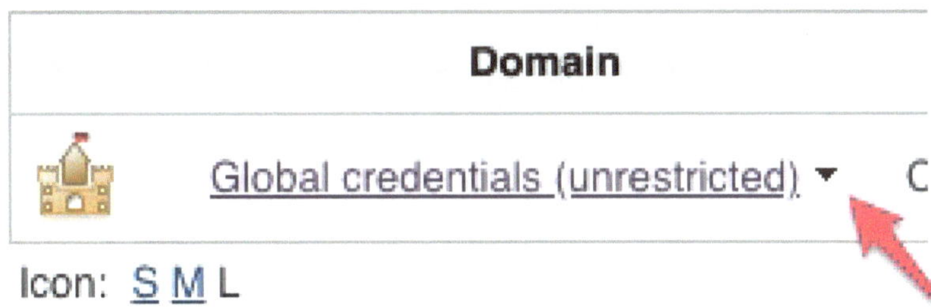

And a drop down will appear where you can choose to add credentials.

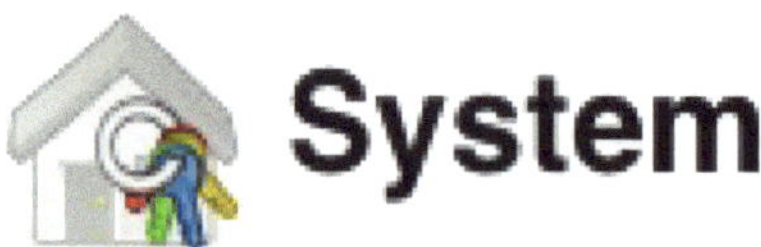

Switch the kind to Secret file, choose your kube config file and give it an ID then click OK.

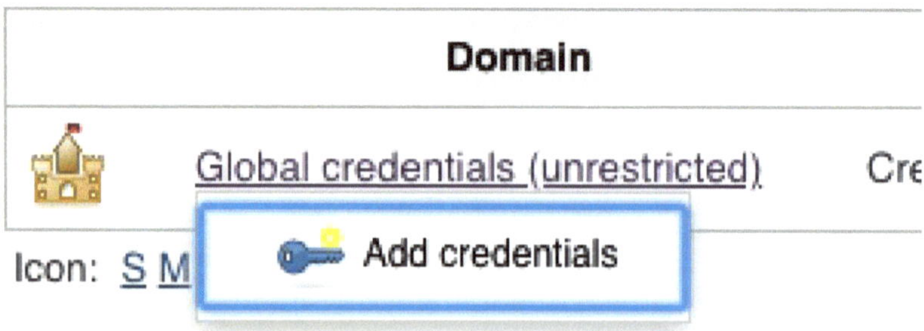

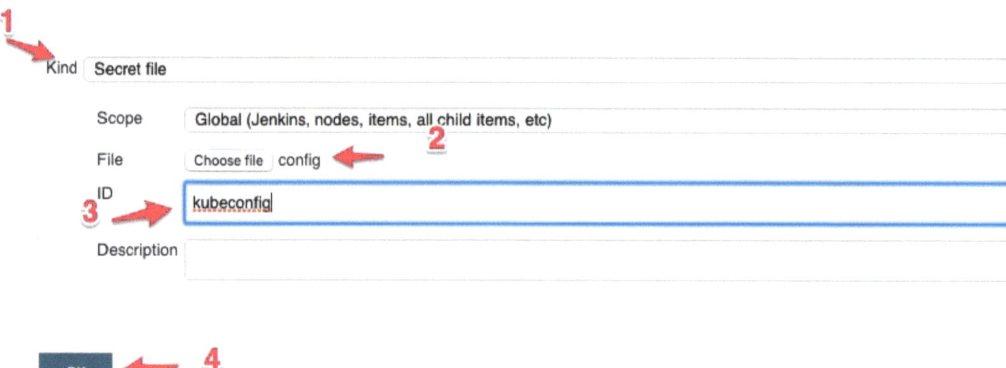

Note the id. It is the credentialId we will use in our withKubeConfig in the Jenkinsfile later.

Create a Job

Let's go ahead now and create our first build job. You can do this by clicking the new item in the left menu or, if you do not have any jobs defined yet, you will also get a link on the main pane.

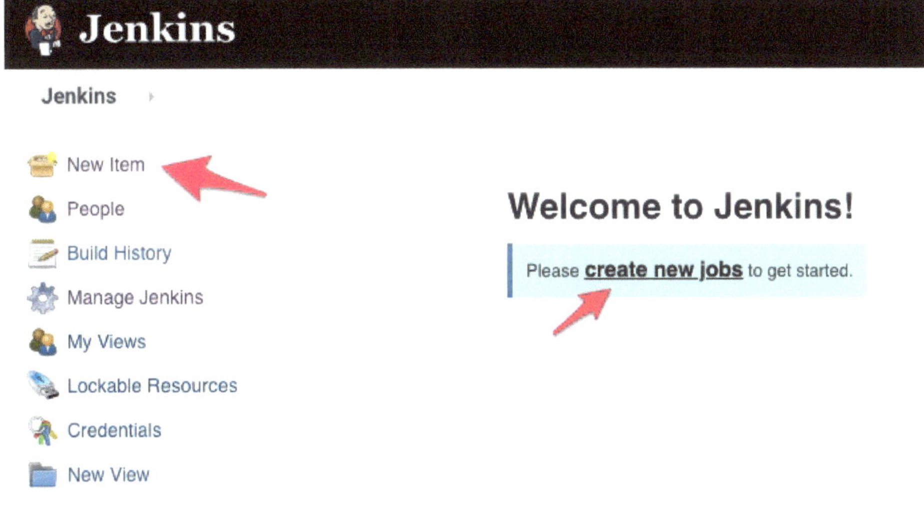

You will land on a page to give the job a name and choose the type of the job

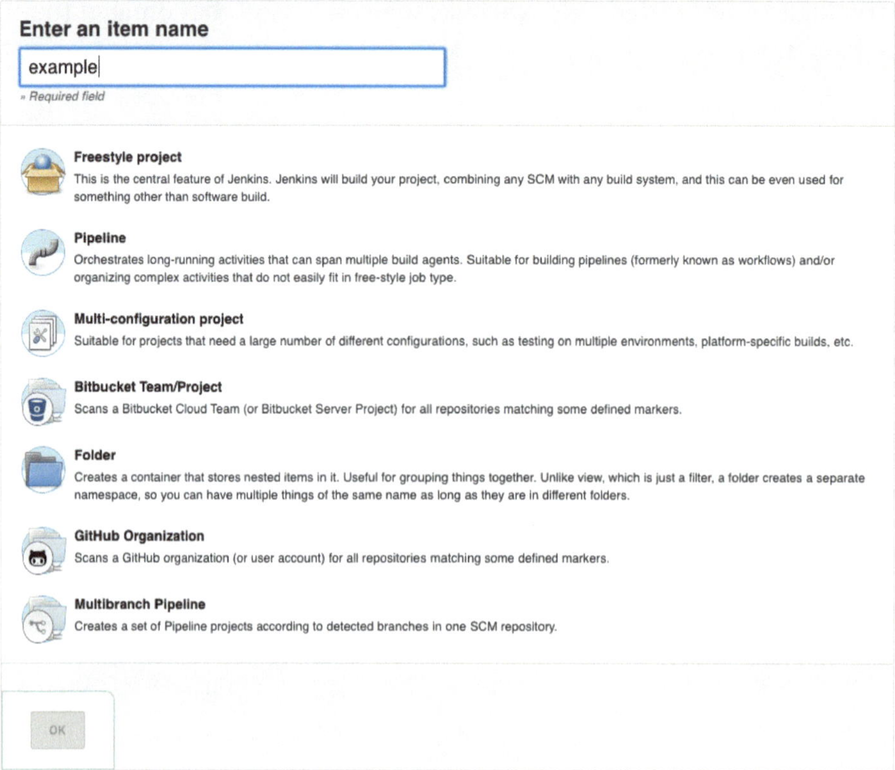

There are many types and each type will give you lots of possibilities so I will not go in details through them all but here is a short summary of what you will get.

- All project types will send you to a new page to configure the job.
- Those pages will be split into different parts.
- Even if some parts are shared like "general" they will vary from one type to another.
- The "Folder" type is actually just a container where you can put other jobs into. It doesn't build anything
- "Bitbucket Team/Project" and "GitHub Organization" will scan the server you connect to and will auto add all repositories that matches criteria you configure. Each repository you add will be set up like a multibranch pipeline. They will need a Jenkinsfile.

- "Freestyle" and "Pipeline" do not support multibranch. You can build multiple branches from those, but they would be seen as part of the same job. This means that the build number will increase even when it is from another branch.
- "Multibranch Pipeline" will handle each branch as separate entities. A new build in a new branch will be marked as build number 1 for the branch. Not next build for the job.

As most developing strategies involves branching, I will only show you how to set up multibranch pipelines. So, from the previous screen, we gave a name and chose Multibranch Pipeline then clicked OK.
Note: The job is now created and exists in Jenkins even if you do not configure anything.

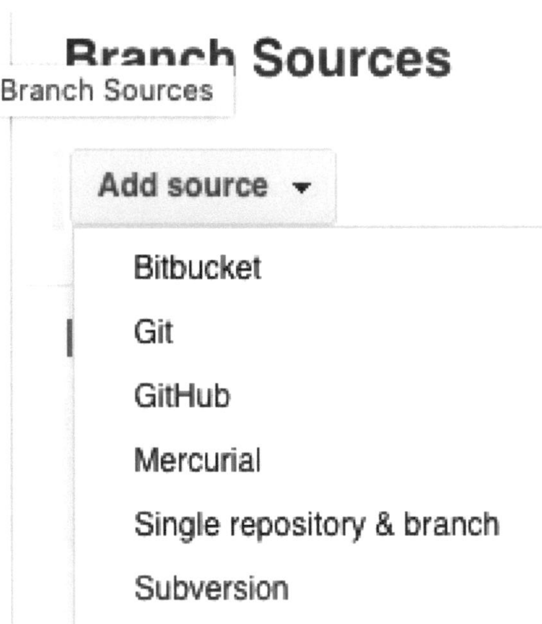

If you choose GitHub or Bitbucket, it will also allow you to fetch the Pull Requests as well. For the others, the concept of PR does not exist so it will not be available.

In every possible choice, you will have the possibility to connect "Credentials", "Behaviors" and "Property strategy" to the source.
Credentials will allow you to connect to a protected resource and will save the login information in Jenkins (can then be reused for another job).

Behaviors has a very long list that vary depending on the type of repository. You can set multiple behaviors for the same source. Some are to fetch PRs, discover tags, filter by name, some configurations for hooks and many checkout behaviors. They all are quite self-explanatory and have a help icon to get more information if you wish. The default is always to discover all branches (and PR for GitHub and Bitbucket) and I usually do not change them.

Property strategy will allow you to set different properties for different branches or have the same for all.

Next step is the Build configuration. The mode is always by Jenkinsfile if you do not have other plugins installed. You will need to add a path to the Jenkinsfile. If you have it in the root of the project, the default is correct. If you called it differently or have placed it in a different folder, update it here.

I would recommend checking the checkbox to run periodically under Scan Multibranch Pipeline Triggers as the automatic is such that it will recheck when it gets another notification of the same SCM (push notifications). But they are unreliable. It will not work in cases where Jenkins is behind a firewall that do not allow it, Jenkins might be down when the notification is sent, some repositories do not send notifications, etc. So, add periodical scan to whatever value seems good for you. I usually set it very low (1 or 2 minutes) because I do not have to wait too long for a build to start. However, you are targeting a GitHub account, you might want to set it higher as it has some quotas per hour. So, you might want to increase the timing.

Orphaned Item Strategy will allow you to discard old items. Either by days or number of items (or both). This is just to clean up some space on your server so you can set it quite high (or not at all) to begin with then lower it over time if you need some space.

If you set them both, it is a logical OR so, let's say you set it with 10 build for 30 days, the build #1 will be cleaned when build #11 is run even if it is the same day; and build #2 will be cleaned even if there are no build #12 if it is older than 30 days.

The rest I leave to the default settings (empty) and click Save. This will trigger a repository scan. It will check the repository you configured to see if it can find a Jenkinsfile on the path and with the name set under Build Configuration. If yes, it will trigger a build for each branch that has the Jenkinsfile. This means that, initially, you might get multiple builds for the different branches.

Building and deploying with NPM

Let's assume that we now have a repository connected to a Jenkins job that we want to build a JavaScript application from. Instead of adding different build capabilities to Jenkins, we will use docker. It is much easier since developers can choose the image they want to use to build without any interventions from operations to add capabilities to Jenkins. We will start our Jenkinsfile with declaring which image we want to use and add some configurations.

```
pipeline {
  agent {
    docker {
      image 'node:12-alpine'
      args '-v /var/lib/jenkins/.npm:/.npm:rw -v /var/lib/jenkins/.npmrc:/.npmrc:ro'
    }
  }

  ...
}
```

The arguments define 2 mounts to the image. One is the npm work directory, so that we can reuse the npm cache throughout multiple builds/jobs. And the second is our configuration for npm, so it uses our private repository. Now let's set up some stages

```
stages {
   stage ('Build') {
     steps {
        sh 'npm install'
     }
   }
   stage ('Test') {
     steps {
        sh 'npm test'
     }
   }
   ...


}
```

Here we run a couple of commands to install dependencies and run the tests. You can run multiple commands inside a step so both could be run inside the same step and you can add as many stages and step as you wish.

This gave you a simple example of what can be done. Now, in this book we want to show how to deploy a containerized application so, let's have a look on how we could build the container and deploy it. First, we will need a Dockerfile to define how we want our container to look like. Here is a simple example to deploy a web application. Note that, in the following example, it is an Angular application that we will deploy but the concept is valid for any web deployment.

```
FROM nginx:alpine
COPY ./dist/ /usr/share/nginx/html/
```

We take the nginx base image and add our built result to the html folder which is the root folder for nginx.

Now, let's see how our Jenkinsfile would look like:

```
def shortCommit
pipeline {
    agent none

    stages {
        agent any
        stage("Get commit hash") {
            steps {
                script {
                    shortCommit = sh(returnStdout: true,
script: "git log -n 1 --pretty=format:'%h'").trim()
                    echo "${shortCommit}"
                }
            }
        }

        stage("Build") {
            agent {
                docker {
                    image 'node:12-alpine'
                    args '-v
/var/lib/jenkins/.npm:/.npm:rw -v
/var/lib/jenkins/.npmrc:/.npmrc:ro'
                }
            }
            steps {
                echo 'Building...'
                sh 'npm install'
                sh 'node_modules/@angular/cli/bin/ng build'
                sh 'npm publish'
            }
        }
```

```
        stage("Publish") {
            agent any
            steps {
                sh "docker build -t
docker.example.com/project/web:${shortCommit} ."
                sh "docker push
docker.example.com/project/web:${shortCommit}"
            }
        }

        stage("Deploy") {
            agent any
            when {
                branch 'release'
            }
            steps {
                withKubeConfig(credentialsId:
'kubeconfig',serverUrl: 'https://k8s.example.com:8443') {
                    sh "kubectl -n namespace set image
deployment web
web=docker.example.com/project/web:${shortCommit}"
                }
            }
        }
    }
}
```

This is a bit more complex and there are some things to note:

1. We define a global variable that will hold the short hash of the commit
   we will build. This is a little trick to pass a common "version" to
   different steps/stages.
2. We start by stating that agent as none. This means that we need to
   define an agent in each stage.
3. First stage is to get the short commit hash that we set in our global
   variable. We also print it out to have it in our log file as well.
4. Next, we have the build stage. Here, we will run it inside of a docker
   container defined by the agent. We choose the right version of node
   for our projects. After we run npm install to get all packages

downloaded. Then ng build; that is Angular CLI to package everything in the dist directory.
5. Publish: We go back to agent any as defined defined in Jenkins and build our container and push it to our private repository. This will force Jenkins to get out of the docker container we had in the previous stage.
6. Notice that we chose to deploy only of we are on the master branch. I mentioned earlier that you can match patterns as well. i.e: to match a branch starting with release- then any number, you would change it to

```
when { branch pattern: "release-\\d+", comparator: "REGEXP" }
```

Any regex will work here.
7. Deployment is done by updating the image tag in the existing deployment in our Kubernetes cluster. This will create a new pod with the new image. You will need to change it accordingly if, for example, you used a DaemonSet instead of a Deployment.
The format is kubectl -n <namespace> set image <deployment|daemonset|replicaset|...> <name of the previous object> <name of container>=<new image tag>

Here is an example of a deployment using this method:

```yaml
apiVersion: apps/v1
kind: Deployment
metadata:
  name: web
  namespace: namespace
  labels:
    app: web
spec:
  selector:
    matchLabels:
      app: web
  replicas: 1
  strategy:
```

```yaml
    type: RollingUpdate
    rollingUpdate:
      maxUnavailable: 25%
  minReadySeconds: 5
  template:
    metadata:
      labels:
        app: identity
    spec:
      containers:
        - image: docker.example.com/project/web:277f867
          imagePullPolicy: Always
          name: identity
          ports:
            - containerPort: 80
          readinessProbe:
            httpGet:
              path: /
              port: 80
            initialDelaySeconds: 5
            periodSeconds: 5
            successThreshold: 1
      imagePullSecrets:
        - name: regcred
```

Note the 2 last lines here. This is how you set credentials for a private repository. To create this secret, run:

```
kubectl -n namespace create secret docker-registry regcred --docker-server=docker.example.com --docker-username=username --docker-password=password --docker-email=kube@example.com
```

Obviously, you will need to create the user in Nexus or use an existing one. I use a specific one here with that I add in a new role that has only read privileges on the docker repositories. The privilege is called nx-repository-view-docker-*-read. You could even specify which docker repository it can access.

Building and deploying with Maven

Much of this is similar to what we just set up for NPM. This is the beauty of our solution. If you have one working, the next is pretty easy to get around.
There are, of course, some changes. We will use a maven image to build and the Dockerfile we use is a bit different. In this example, I will use a Spring Boot application. This creates a runnable jar file. Any other application with a single runnable jar file would be exactly the same (except maybe the port to expose in the Dockerfile).

So, first, here is our Dockerfile:

```
FROM openjdk:11-jre-slim
ARG JAR_FILE=target/*.jar
ADD ${JAR_FILE} /app.jar
EXPOSE 8080
CMD ["java","-Djava.security.egd=file:/dev/./urandom","-jar","/app.jar"]
```

In short, we take a java base image, you might want to change the tag if you are running on a different Java version. Create the argument that are our built jar file and copy it to the container. We expose the port 8080 that our application is running on and start it with a simple java -jar command.

You might want to set a different user to run the application. Simply create it and set it with USER in the :

```
FROM openjdk:11-jre-slim
RUN addgroup -S spring && adduser -S spring -G spring
USER spring:spring
ARG JAR_FILE=target/*.jar
…
```

This will run your application as the spring user.

Now let's see our Jenkinsfile

```
def shortCommit
pipeline {
    agent none

    stages {
        stage("Get commit hash") {
            agent any
            steps {
                script {
                    shortCommit = sh(returnStdout: true,
script: "git log -n 1 --pretty=format:'%h'").trim()
                    echo "${shortCommit}"
                }
            }
        }

        stage("Build") {
            agent {
                docker {
                    image 'maven:3-jdk-11'
                    args "-v ${HUDSON_HOME}/.m2:/.m2:rw -e
MAVEN_CONFIG=/.m2 -e MAVEN_OPTS=-Duser.home=/"
                }
            }
            steps {
                echo 'Building...'
                sh 'mvn clean deploy -Pcloud'
            }
        }

        stage("Publish") {
            agent any
            steps {
                sh "docker build -t
docker.example.com/example/demo-app:${shortCommit} ."
                sh "docker push
docker.example.com/example/demo-app:${shortCommit}"
            }
```

```
                }

        stage("Deploy") {
            agent any
            steps {
                withKubeConfig(credentialsId:
'kubeconfig',serverUrl: 'https://k8s.example.com:8443') {
                    sh "kubectl -n namespace set image
deployment demo-app demo-
app=docker.example.com/example/demo-app:${shortCommit}"
                }
            }
        }
    }
}
```

The differences from NPM is the image we use. Here we need an image that has maven capabilities and the volume we mount is the configuration for maven instead of NPM. This has a big advantage as it will not need to download all maven dependencies every time you run a new build as they already would be in the .m2 directory. On a clean image, this would be empty. I also set the maven options for user home as it will then guaranty that the correct setting.xml is loaded ad, depending on the image you use, it may vary.

Building image without Docker installed

I also wanted to show you an alternative way of building the docker image. There is a tool called JIB that we can use as a maven or Gradle plugin that do not require the docker daemon to run. This means that we can deploy the docker image from the maven command inside our maven build container. It also has the advantage that the base image (gcr.io/distroless/java) used is quite small so our resulting image will be smaller (around 20 MB) than when we use openjdk images. It is also highly configurable. You can change the base image, how the container is created, add extra directories, even change the type of image to OCI.

Just add the plugin in your pom.xml

```xml
<build>
    <finalName>demo-app</finalName>
    <plugins>
        <plugin>
            <groupId>pl.project13.maven</groupId>
            <artifactId>git-commit-id-plugin</artifactId>
            <version>3.0.1</version>
            <executions>
                <execution>
                    <id>get-the-git-infos</id>
                    <goals>
                        <goal>revision</goal>
                    </goals>
                </execution>
                <execution>
                    <id>validate-the-git-infos</id>
                    <goals>
                        <goal>validateRevision</goal>
                    </goals>
                </execution>
            </executions>
        </plugin>
        <plugin>
            <groupId>com.google.cloud.tools</groupId>
            <artifactId>jib-maven-plugin</artifactId>
            <version>2.1.0</version>
            <configuration>
                <to>
                    <image>docker.example.com/example/demo-app:${git.commit.id.abbrev}</image>
                    <tags>
                        <tag>latest</tag>
                    </tags>
                </to>
            </configuration>
            <executions>
                <execution>
                    <id>build</id>
```

```xml
                <phase>deploy</phase>
                <goals>
                    <goal>build</goal>
                </goals>
            </execution>
        </executions>
    </plugin>
</plugins>
</build>
```

We also add the git-commit-id-plugin so that we can set the tag of the image the same way we did in our Jenkinsfile (short hash of the git commit). The configuration is quite simple here as we use lot of the defaults. This will create and push the image to our private registry. However, we need to define authentication for the plugin. It does not use docker daemon so it will not use the authentication provided by docker. The trick here is to add a server to your settings.xml

```xml
<server>
   <id>docker.example.com</id>
   <username>username</username>
   <password>password</password>
</server>
```

The id must match the host URL as set in the plugin.

One more thing we do need to add is adding the .cache volume mount to our Jenkinsfile (-v ${HUDSON_HOME}/.cache:/.cache) so we can also use the same cache for multiple build. The agent part of the pipeline will then look like this:

```
agent {
    docker {
        image 'maven:3-jdk-11'
        args "-v ${HUDSON_HOME}/.m2:/.m2:rw -v ${HUDSON_HOME}/.cache:/.cache -e MAVEN_CONFIG=/.m2 -e MAVEN_OPTS=-Duser.home=/"
```

        }
}

If you do not set it, you will get an error in the build that actually will be very silent. This is just because the process building the image does not have enough rights to create /.cache directory. If you did not change the user home, it should not be a problem and you would only have to add it if you want to share the cache between builds.

Recommended plugins

I want to underline that Jenkins has well over 1000 integrations. Look at the plugin manager and you will probably find some that might help you in your daily workflow. On the other hand, there are so many that you might get lost and it is not always easy to know if a plugin is a good one or not.
In any case, always check the last update for a plugin before installing it. If it hasn't been updated in years, skip it.
To help you on the way, I have a short list of plugins I use that I believe many people might enjoy.

Global Slack Notifier

It requires to also install the Slack Notification plugin as well. This will allow you to add global notifications after each job is ran. You can setup trigger for the different statuses (success, failed, etc.) and messages for each status. This will also allow you to use slackSend directive in your pipelines. It is registered as an app in Slack as well so you just need to go to https://my.slack.com/services/new/jenkins-ci and it will guide you through the installation process.

SonarQube Scanner for Jenkins

If you have a SonarQube server (or multiples), this is a nice plugin to connect to it (or them). It will allow you to use environment variables so, it you wish to add a scan to one of your steps just add mvn $SONAR_MAVEN_GOAL in it and it will fetch the configuration from Jenkins.

vSphere

If you are coming from my previous book, you probably have an available vSphere infrastructure. This plugin will allow you to create Jenkins agents from VM template on demand.

JIRA Pipeline Steps

If you wish to do some updates in Jira based on a build, this is a plugin you might like. It can basically do anything available in the Jira API. From search, creating issues, updating them, create a new release, etc.

Conclusion

We have now shown how to setup Nexus and Jenkins to build and hold your artifacts privately from your source code on Linux machines. This, assuming that you have some available resources, will just cost you a bit of time to set up and a minimal amount to maintain.

You can easily change Nexus to Artifactory, but, remember that, if you wish to hold Docker images, you will need to pay for the feature in Artifactory.

You can also change Jenkins to another build server. Now that GitHub offer a free plan for an organization, you might think that Travis-CI is a good alternative, but you will still need to subscribe to get private repositories built there. Starting at $69/month it still can be a good fit for you.

References

Nexus: https://www.sonatype.com/nexus-repository-oss
Artifactory OSS: https://jfrog.com/open-source/
Jenkins: https://jenkins.io/
JIB: https://github.com/GoogleContainerTools/jib

Acknowledgement

I just want to take a moment to thanks my wife Christel for her patience throughout this work as well as the help and support that she gave me. Thanks you very much.